ITALIAN COOKING

Mary Reynolds

GOLDEN PRESS / NEW YORK
Western Publishing Company, Inc.
Racine, Wisconsin

CONTENTS

Sauces 12

Soups & Appetizers 18

Pasta, Rice & Pizzas 28

Meat 40

Poultry 56

Fish & Shellfish 66

Vegetables & Salads 72

Desserts 82

Index 94

NOTES:

Always preheat the oven to the specified temperature.

Margarine can be substited for butter in all recipes

If substituting dried herbs for fresh, use a third of the amount;
if substituting fresh for dried, use 3 times the amount.

This edition prepared under the supervision of
Joanna Morris

This edition published 1984 by Golden Press
Library of Congress Catalog Card Number: 84-80343
ISBN 0-307-09960-1
Golden® and Golden Press® are registered trademarks
of Western Publishing Company, Inc.

First published in 1981 in the U.K. by Cathay Books,
59 Grosvenor Street, London W1

© 1984, 1982, 1981 Cathay Books

Printed in Hong Kong

INTRODUCTION

The best cooking in Italy is found in the home. Italian women take pleasure in shopping for the best quality ingredients and in cooking attractive meals for their families.

The main meal of the day is an important event, a social occasion when all the family gather around the table to exchange the news and gossip of the day and to share in the enjoyment of "mama's" cooking. A traditional Italian meal – although infinitely flexible – generally consists of a *minestra* (soup, pasta dish or risotto), followed by a course of meat, fish or poultry with one or two vegetables. Sometimes a salad is served after the main course. The meal ends with cheese and fresh fruit in season, and is rounded off with a small cup of strong espresso. On special occasions an antipasto may be served before the *minestra* and a dessert before the fruit.

Generally speaking, hard and fast rules have no place in the Italian kitchen, so use the recipes in this book as guidelines, always testing and adapting as you go along.

Italian Regional Cooking

Until 1861, Italy was a collection of independent states, each with its own laws, customs and traditions. Today, as you travel from one area to another, you will notice regional differences between the landscape, people, dialects and, of course, foods.

There is a particularly marked difference between northern and southern Italy. The regions in the north tend to be more industrial and prosperous than those in the poorer south and the northern soil tends to be more fertile. The differences as far as cooking is concerned are that the traditional northern pasta is the flat variety, freshly made with eggs, and the fat used for cooking is generally butter. In southern Italy, tubular varieties of pasta are more common and olive oil is used for cooking. Flavors are much stronger in the south because of the extensive use of fresh herbs and spices, particularly in the sauces.

Well-known pasta dishes of the northern province of Liguria include ravioli and minestrone soup. The rice-growing area in the Po Valley, just behind Venice, provides abundant supplies of arborio rice. This especially absorbent medium-grained rice is available in specialty food stores and is the basis for risottos. Many delicious, creamy risotto recipes have evolved; risotto Milanese from Lombardy is one of the best known.

Two of the most famous products of the north are Parmesan cheese and prosciutto ham, both from Parma. Parmesan cheese is at its best after 2 years of drying and maturing, and gets stronger the older it becomes. The whey from the cheese is fed to the Parma pigs and, combined with the careful salting and drying processes on the hillsides, results in the delicately flavored ham.

Italy is surrounded on three sides by sea and locally caught fish are a dominant feature of most regional cuisines. Venice is particularly noted for its red and gray mullet, squid, scampi and mussels. In the north, deep-sea fish are supplemented by excellent freshwater fish from the lakes of Lombardy – especially eels. The southern coast and the islands of Sicily and Sardinia are dotted with fishing villages. Here, tuna, sardines, swordfish and a variety of shellfish are caught and used locally in pasta dishes, sauces, soups, stews and salads.

Abundant local supplies of tomatoes, garlic, herbs and anchovies in the southern regions give dishes their characteristic aromatic quality. Naples, the culinary center of the south, claims the invention of the pizza and ice cream as we

know them today. Pizzas are baked in open-brick ovens of pizzerias and bakeries, and are most often eaten as snacks. Mozzarella, the cheese used for pizza topping, has been made for centuries in the surrounding countryside of Campania. It is an ideal "melting" cheese and lends itself to all types of pizzas and cooked dishes. The equally famous Italian ices are made in mouth-watering flavors and, like the pizza, have become very popular all over Italy and around the world.

Italy is the world's largest wine producer and almost every region makes its contribution to the great variety of exported table wines. Piemonte is the home of Barolo, a fine red to serve with roast meat and game, and the modest but flavorsome Barbera, an ideal wine to drink with robust pasta dishes and pizzas. Veneto provides two popular wines: the dry, red Valpolicella and Soave – a medium white wine. From Tuscany comes the deservedly famous Chianti Classico, the perfect accompaniment to roasts, broiled meats and game. Other Italian wines worth trying are Orvieto, Verdicchio, Frascati and Lambrusco.

Italian Ingredients

Delicatessens and supermarkets sell a wide variety of Italian ingredients.

CHEESES

Parmesan: A unique cheese, grated and added to sauces, pasta, rice and other dishes to give an incomparable flavor. Buy it in chunks and grate it at home. Bottles of pre-grated Parmesan cannot compare with freshly grated.

Mozzarella: A white cheese, used extensively in cooking for its melting properties, especially as a topping for pizzas. It is sold in packages but, when bought fresh, is moist and dripping with whey. Bel Paese can be used as a substitute.

Ricotta: A soft, white cheese, made from whey. Must be eaten absolutely fresh. Used in stuffings and sweet fillings.

Gorgonzola: The famous Italian blue-veined table cheese. When ripe, it should be mild and soft.

Other Italian cheeses to look for are Bel Paese, Romano, Fontina, Provolone and Cacciocavallo.

CURED MEATS AND SAUSAGES

Prosciutto: Delicately cured ham, eaten smoked and wafer thin. The best comes from Parma or San Daniele. No real substitute, but for cooked dishes use cooked ham.

Salami: Long dry-cured sausages of lean ground meat with pork fat and spices. There are various types, of which Salami Milano is considered the best. Serve sliced in mixed antipasti, chopped in stuffings.

Mortadella: Large smooth-textured cooked pork sausage laced with pork fat and spices. Serve sliced for antipasti, chopped in stuffings.

Cotechino: Lightly cured pork sausage, weighing from 1 to 2 lb. First it is boiled, then thickly sliced and served with lentils or beans, or cold with salad.

Luganega: Long, thin coiled sausage of mild, coarsely ground pork. Also called *Salsiccia*. Fry, broil or boil and serve hot with lentils or potatoes.

HERBS

Herbs are an essential flavoring in many Italian dishes. Fresh herbs are normally used in Italy. It is well worth growing the herbs you cannot buy in pots on the window sill or in the garden. Use dried herbs when fresh are unavailable, but replace dried herbs regularly to avoid staleness. The following herbs are used most commonly in Italian cooking.

Basil: The incomparable herb for tomato dishes. Also popular in salads, sauces and soups.

Bay Leaves: As a flavoring for casseroles, stews, soups and roasts.

Oregano: An ingredient used in many dishes, especially pizzas, casseroles and sauces.

Parsley: The universal herb for flavoring Italian dishes. Italian parsley is the flat-leaved variety, so use this when available.

Rosemary: Strongly-flavored herb, used mainly for roast lamb or pork. Also used in chicken and fish dishes.

Sage: Especially good for flavoring veal and chicken dishes cooked in wine.

CUPBOARD INGREDIENTS

The following non-perishable ingredients are frequently used in Italian dishes and it is useful to keep a stock of them on hand.

Pasta: Available in an immense variety of shapes and used in many different ways: both the shaped pastas of the south (macaroni, spaghetti, ziti, bucatini, rigatoni, etc) and the lighter, flat egg pastas of the north (tagliatelle, fettuccine, lasagne, etc). Keep a variety of different kinds of pasta on hand – including a few of the less usual shapes and small varieties for soups.

Rice: Italian arborio rice is thick and short and absorbs more liquid than other types of rice. It is used to make creamy risotto. Occasionally available in specialty food stores.

Beans: Dried beans and lentils, canned white cannellini and red kidney beans are used for soups, salads and other dishes.

Pepper and Salt: Italians always use freshly ground black peppercorns from a pepper mill and, when possible, coarse sea salt.

Wine Vinegar: Essential for salad dressings and used in many other recipes.

Olive and Vegetable Oils: The distinctive flavor of good olive oil is needed for salad dressings and for general cooking because olive oil gives the dish a special character. Otherwise, ground nut or sunflower oils are suitable.

Anchovy Fillets in Oil: For adding zest to sauces, pizzas and antipasti dishes.

Capers: Small capers add authenticity to many sauces, fish dishes and garnishes.

Olives: Keep small bottles of green, ripe and stuffed olives on hand, but buy fresh loose olives when possible since their flavor is much better.

Canned Tomatoes: Italian plum, crushed and whole peeled tomatoes have an excellent flavor and are time-saving and convenient to use for sauces and casseroles.

Tomato Paste: Small amounts are invaluable for strengthening the flavor and color of dishes in which fresh or canned tomatoes are used.

Fortified Wines: Dry white vermouth can be used in recipes calling for dry white wine and herbs. Marsala adds a richness to veal, poultry and ham dishes.

SAUCES

Chicken Liver Sauce
Salsa di Fegatini

4 tablespoons butter
1 small onion, chopped
½ cup finely chopped mushrooms
½ lb chicken livers, diced
1 tablespoon flour
2 tablespoons Marsala
1¼ cups Chicken Broth (page 19)
1 tablespoon tomato paste
4 slices bacon, cooked and crumbled
Salt and pepper

Melt 3 tablespoons of the butter in a large saucepan. Add the onion and sauté for 6 to 8 minutes, stirring occasionally. Increase the heat and add the mushrooms and chicken livers. Sauté, stirring, for 2 minutes. Add the flour and continue stirring for 1 minute.

Add the Marsala, then stir in the broth, tomato paste, bacon and a little salt and pepper. Bring to a boil, cover and simmer for 30 to 40 minutes. Stir in the remaining butter and check the seasoning.

Serve with any kind of pasta.

Makes about 2 cups

Meat Sauce
Salsa di Carne

4 slices bacon, diced
1 tablespoon butter
1 onion, chopped
1 carrot, diced
1 stalk celery, diced
¾ lb lean ground beef
2 tablespoons flour
2 cups beef broth
1 tablespoon tomato paste
Salt and pepper
Grated nutmeg

Sauté the bacon in a large saucepan until crisp. Add the butter, onion, carrot and celery and cook over low heat for 10 minutes, stirring frequently. Add the meat and continue stirring until browned. Stir in the flour and cook for 2 minutes. Stir in the broth and tomato paste and season to taste with salt, pepper and nutmeg. Bring to a boil, cover and simmer for 1 hour, stirring occasionally.

Serve with any kind of pasta.
Makes about 3 cups

Rich Meat Sauce
Ragù Bolognese

4 slices bacon, diced
1 tablespoon butter
1 onion, finely chopped
1 carrot, diced
1 stalk celery, diced
¾ lb lean ground beef
¼ lb chicken livers, chopped
¼ cup dry vermouth or white wine
1¼ cups beef broth
1 tablespoon tomato paste
Salt and pepper
Grated nutmeg
2 tablespoons light cream

Sauté the bacon in a large saucepan until crisp. Add the butter, onion, carrot and celery and cook over low heat, stirring frequently. Add the meat and cook, stirring, until browned. Stir in the chicken livers and the vermouth. Bring to a boil and simmer rapidly until the liquid has almost completely evaporated.

Stir in the broth and tomato paste and season to taste with salt, pepper and nutmeg. Bring to a boil, cover and simmer for 1 hour, stirring occasionally. Check the seasoning and stir in the cream.

Serve with tagliatelli, spaghetti or other pasta.
Makes about 2½ cups

Tomato Sauce
Salsa di Pomodori

1 can (16 oz) crushed tomatoes
1 onion, chopped
1 clove garlic, crushed
1 carrot, sliced
1 stalk celery, diced
2 teaspoons tomato paste
1 teaspoon sugar
Salt and pepper
¾ teaspoon dried basil

Combine the tomatoes, onion, garlic, carrot, celery, tomato paste and sugar in a saucepan. Bring to a boil, partially cover and simmer for 30 minutes. Stir in salt and pepper to taste.

Puree in a blender. Return to the pan and simmer until thickened. Stir in the basil and check the seasoning.

Serve with pasta or meat dishes.
Makes about 1¼ cups

Fresh Tomato Sauce

Salsa Pizzaiola

2 tablespoons olive
oil
2 cloves garlic,
minced
1½ lb ripe tomatoes,
chopped
1 teaspoon sugar
Salt and pepper
1 tablespoon
chopped basil,
oregano or parsley

Heat the oil in a medium-size saucepan. Add the garlic and sauté until
softened, about 2 minutes. Add the
tomatoes and sugar. Simmer briskly
for a few minutes until most of the
liquid has evaporated and the tomatoes are softened. Pass through a food
mill; season with salt and pepper.

Garnish with the herbs and serve
with steaks, chops, fish or pasta.
Makes about 2 cups

15

Béchamel Sauce
Besciamella

3 tablespoons butter
6 tablespoons flour
2½ cups hot milk
Salt and pepper
Grated nutmeg

Melt the butter in a small saucepan. Add the flour and cook, stirring, for 1 minute. Remove from the heat and gradually stir in the milk.

Return to the heat and cook, stirring, until thickened. Simmer for 3 minutes. Season to taste with salt, pepper and nutmeg.

Makes about 2½ cups

NOTE: For additional flavor, add a bay leaf to the milk before heating. Remove before adding to the sauce.

Mayonnaise
Maionese

2 egg yolks
½ teaspoon salt
2 to 3 teaspoons
   lemon juice
¾ to 1 cup olive oil

Have all the ingredients at room temperature.

Beat the egg yolks in a small bowl. Add the salt and 1 teaspoon of the lemon juice and beat. Add the oil drop by drop, beating constantly, until the sauce becomes thick and shiny. Add the remaining oil in a thin stream, beating constantly. Add lemon juice to taste.

Makes about 1¼ cups

Tuna Mayonnaise
Maionese Tonnata

1 cup Mayonnaise
  (opposite)
1 can (3½ oz) tuna
3 anchovy fillets
1 tablespoon lemon
  juice

Place the mayonnaise in a blender.
Add the undrained tuna, anchovy and
lemon juice; puree until smooth.

Serve with hard-cooked eggs as an
appetizer or over cold sliced chicken,
turkey or veal.

Makes about 1¼ cups

Piquant Green Sauce
Salsa Verde

2 shallots
1 clove garlic
1 gherkin
1 tablespoon capers
½ cup chopped
  parsley
2 tablespoons lemon
  juice
6 tablespoons olive
  oil
Salt and pepper

Place all the ingredients in a blender
and puree until smooth.

Or finely chop the first five ingredients together. Stir in the lemon juice
and oil and season to taste with salt and
pepper.

Serve with hot or cold meat, fish or
poultry.

Makes about 1 cup

SOUPS & APPETIZERS

Roman Egg Soup
Stracciatella

2 eggs
2 tablespoons fine
   semolina
½ cup grated
   Parmesan cheese
6 cups Chicken
   Broth (opposite)

Beat together the eggs, semolina, cheese and about 1 cup of the chicken broth. Bring the remaining broth to a boil in a large saucepan. Immediately remove from the heat and beat in the egg mixture.

.Continue beating over low heat for 2 to 3 minutes, just until the eggs break into ragged flakes. Serve immediately.
4 to 6 servings

Chicken Broth

Brodo di Pollo

This forms the basis of many soups and sauces. The chicken can be served hot for the main course, or cold with Piquant Green Sauce or Tuna Mayonnaise (both on page 17).

1 stewing chicken
   (3 to 4 lb)
2 quarts water
1 carrot, sliced
1 onion, sliced
2 stalks celery, sliced
2 tomatoes,
   quartered
1 bay leaf
6 peppercorns

Place the chicken and giblets (except the liver) in a stock pot and add the water. Bring to a boil and skim off the top. Add the vegetables, bay leaf and peppercorns. Cover and simmer gently for about 4 hours, or until the chicken is tender. Remove the chicken. Strain the broth; season to taste.

Makes about 2 quarts

Cheese Noodles in Broth
Passatelli in Brodo

---

5 cups Chicken Broth (page 19)
1 egg, beaten
2 teaspoons flour
¼ cup grated Parmesan cheese
⅓ cup dry white bread crumbs
1 tablespoon butter, softened
Pepper
Grated nutmeg

Bring the chicken broth to a boil in a large saucepan.

Place the egg, flour, cheese, bread crumbs and butter in a bowl. Add the pepper and nutmeg and work to a firm paste.

Press through a food mill or metal colander directly into the boiling broth. Simmer until the noodles rise to the surface, about 2 minutes.

Pour into individual soup bowls and serve immediately with additional Parmesan cheese.

4 to 6 servings

Zucchini Soup
Zuppa di Zucchini

---

3 tablespoons butter
1 onion, sliced
1 lb zucchini, thinly sliced
5 cups Chicken Broth (page 19)
2 small eggs
2 tablespoons grated Parmesan cheese
1 tablespoon chopped parsley
2 teaspoons chopped basil
Salt and pepper
Crostini (below)

Melt the butter in a large saucepan. Add the onion and cook for 5 minutes. Add the zucchini and cook, stirring frequently, for 5 to 10 minutes. Add the chicken broth and bring to a boil. Cover and simmer for 20 minutes.

Puree in a blender. Return to the saucepan and bring back to a boil.

Beat the eggs, cheese and herbs together in a bowl. Slowly stir in the boiling soup. Add salt and pepper to taste and ladle into soup bowls. Garnish with the crostini and serve immediately.

4 to 6 servings

CROSTINI: Toast bread slices on one side in a hot oven. Spread the untoasted side with butter and sprinkle with grated cheese. Place under a hot broiler until golden and bubbling. Cut into cubes.

Omelet Soup
Minestra di Frittata

5 cups Chicken
  Broth (page 19)
2 eggs
1 tablespoon flour
¼ cup milk
Salt and pepper
Oil
¼ cup grated
  Parmesan cheese

Bring the chicken broth to a boil in a large saucepan.

Beat the eggs with the flour, milk and a little salt and pepper.

Heat a little oil in a skillet over high heat. When very hot, pour in the eggs and cook for about 1 minute, or until set. Tip out of the pan, roll up and cut into thin strips. Add to the boiling broth with the cheese. Serve immediately. Sprinkle with chopped parsley if desired.
4 to 6 servings

Thick Vegetable Soup
Minestrone

½ lb cabbage
1 large onion
1 large carrot
2 stalks celery
2 zucchini
3 tomatoes, peeled
4 slices bacon
2 tablespoons oil
2 cloves garlic,
  chopped
2 quarts water
¼ teaspoon dried
  basil
½ cup uncooked rice
2 tablespoons
  chopped parsley
2 tablespoons grated
  Parmesan cheese
Salt and pepper

Shred the cabbage; chop the other vegetables and the bacon.

Heat the oil in a large saucepan. Add the bacon, onion, carrot, celery and garlic and cook over low heat, stirring frequently, for about 10 minutes.

Add the water and bring to a boil. Add the cabbage, zucchini, tomatoes, basil and rice. Simmer gently for 20 minutes. Stir in the parsley, cheese and salt and pepper to taste.

Serve with additional Parmesan cheese and crusty bread.

6 servings

NOTE: Small pasta may be used instead of rice.

Assorted Antipasto
Antipasti Misti

3 tomatoes, sliced
3 tablespoons olive
  oil
1 teaspoon chopped
  basil
Salt and pepper
1 fennel bulb
1 teaspoon lemon
  juice
1 clove garlic,
  minced
6 slices Italian
  salami
6 slices garlic
  sausage
½ cup ripe olives
2 hard-cooked eggs,
  quartered

Arrange the tomato slices at one end of a platter. Sprinkle with 1 tablespoon of the oil, the basil and salt and pepper to taste.

Trim the fennel, cut lengthwise into thin slices, then into strips. Mix the remaining oil with the lemon juice, garlic and salt and pepper to taste. Add the fennel and toss well. Arrange at the other end of the platter.

Arrange the salami and garlic sausage in the middle of the platter. Top with the olives and eggs. Garnish with basil or parsley.

4 servings

Home-Style Antipasto

Antipasto alla Casalinga

2 green peppers
3 tablespoons olive oil
2 teaspoons red wine vinegar
Salt and pepper
4 tomatoes, sliced
Few thinly sliced onion rings
1 can (7 oz) tuna, drained and flaked
2 cans (3¾ oz each) sardines in oil, drained
¼ cup Mayonnaise (page 16)

Char the peppers under a preheated broiler, turning frequently. Cut in half and rinse under cold water to remove the skin and seeds. Pat dry and finely slice. Mix with 2 tablespoons of the oil, the vinegar and a little salt. Refrigerate. (Bring to room temperature before serving.)

Season the tomato slices with salt and pepper and sprinkle with the remaining oil. Arrange the pepper slices on a platter and top with the tomatoes. Scatter the onion rings over the top. Place the tuna in the center and surround with the sardines. Serve with mayonnaise.

4 servings

Marinated Artichoke Hearts
Carciofi alla Borghese

1 clove garlic,
   crushed
1½ tablespoons
   lemon juice
4½ tablespoons
   olive oil
Salt and pepper
1 bay leaf
16 fresh cooked or
   canned artichoke
   hearts
1 tablespoon
   chopped parsley

Beat together the garlic, lemon juice, oil and salt and pepper to taste in a bowl. Add the bay leaf and artichoke hearts and stir gently. Cover and chill for about 2 hours, stirring occasionally. Discard the bay leaf.

Divide the artichokes among serving dishes. Spoon the marinade over and sprinkle with parsley.

4 servings

Eggplant Appetizer
Caponata

1 large eggplant
Salt
4 stalks celery
6 tablespoons olive
   oil
Salt and pepper
1 large onion,
   chopped
1 can (16 oz) crushed
   tomatoes
1 tablespoon tomato
   paste
2 to 3 tablespoons
   red wine vinegar
2 tablespoons sugar
2 tablespoons capers
12 pitted green
   olives

Cut the eggplant into ½-inch cubes. Sprinkle with salt, place in a colander and let stand for 1 hour. Pat dry.

Cook the celery in boiling water for 6 to 8 minutes. Drain and cut into ½-inch pieces.

Heat 4 tablespoons of the oil in a large skillet. Add the eggplant and sauté quickly, stirring frequently, for about 10 minutes, or until tender. Season to taste with salt and pepper.

Heat the remaining oil in a large saucepan. Add the onion and cook for 5 minutes. Add the celery and cook, stirring, for 5 minutes. Add the tomatoes, tomato paste and a little salt and pepper. Simmer gently for about 5 minutes, or until the celery and onion are tender.

Add 2 tablespoons vinegar, the sugar, capers, olives and eggplant. Simmer for a few minutes, stirring. Adjust the seasoning and add extra vinegar if necessary. Cool, cover and chill until ready to serve. Garnish with pignoli and wedges of hard-cooked egg.

4 to 6 servings

Mushroom and Shrimp Salad
Insalata di Funghi e Gamberi

6 tablespoons olive oil
2 tablespoons lemon juice
Pepper
1 clove garlic
2 lb mushrooms, thinly sliced
½ teaspoon salt
1 tablespoon chopped parsley
½ lb shelled cooked tiny shrimp

Beat the oil, lemon juice and a little pepper in a bowl. Add the garlic and mushrooms and stir gently. Cover and chill for at least 1 hour.

Stir in the salt and parsley. Spoon into a serving dish and top with the shrimp.

4 servings

NOTE: Very fresh mushrooms and good olive oil are essential for this recipe.

Eggs with Tuna Mayonnaise
Uova Sode Tonnata

4 hard-cooked eggs
Tuna Mayonnaise
(page 17)
4 anchovy fillets
Few capers

Cut the eggs in half lengthwise and arrange cut-side down on a platter or individual dishes. Coat with the mayonnaise.

Cut the anchovy fillets in half lengthwise and curl one strip on top of each egg half. Sprinkle with the capers. Garnish with parsley.

4 servings

Prosciutto with Figs
Prosciutto e Fichi

8 ripe figs
4 slices prosciutto

Cut each fig into quarters almost to the bottom. Arrange the prosciutto on individual plates and top with figs.

4 servings

Prosciutto with Melon
Prosciutto con Melone

1 sweet ripe melon,
chilled
4 slices prosciutto

Cut the melon into quarters and remove the seeds. Wrap the prosciutto over the melon. Serve with freshly ground black pepper.

4 servings

PASTA, RICE & PIZZAS

Country-Style Rice
Risotto alla Paesana

3 tablespoons olive oil
1 onion, chopped
2 stalks celery, thinly sliced
1 zucchini, thinly sliced
½ package (10-oz size) frozen lima beans
1½ cups chicken broth
1⅓ cups instant rice
2 tablespoons butter
¼ lb cooked ham, cut into strips
¼ cup grated Parmesan cheese
Salt and pepper

Heat the oil in a large heavy-based saucepan. Add the onion and celery and sauté for 3 minutes. Stir in the zucchini and beans. Cover and steam over medium heat for 5 minutes. Add the broth and bring to a boil.

Stir in the rice. Cover and remove from the heat. Let stand for 10 minutes, or until the liquid is absorbed. Fluff the rice with a fork. Stir in the butter, ham, cheese and salt and pepper to taste.

Spoon into a warmed serving dish and serve immediately with additional Parmesan cheese.

4 servings

Rice with Meat Sauce
Risotto con Ragù

1½ cups chicken broth
1 tablespoon oil
4 tablespoons butter
1 onion, finely chopped
1⅓ cups instant rice
¼ cup grated Parmesan cheese
Salt and pepper
Chicken Liver Sauce or Meat Sauce (pages 12 and 13)

Bring the chicken broth to a boil in a small saucepan.

Heat the oil and half the butter in a heavy medium-size saucepan. Add the onion and sauté until soft. Add the rice and cook, stirring, for 1 minute.

Add the hot broth, stir well and remove from the heat. Let stand for 5 minutes. Stir in the remaining butter, the cheese and salt and pepper to taste. Fluff the rice with a fork.

Spoon into a warmed serving dish and serve with sauce and additional Parmesan.

4 servings

Homemade Egg Pasta
Pasta all' Uovo

2 cups all-purpose
  flour
2 large eggs
2 teaspoons oil
½ teaspoon salt
3 tablespoons water
  (approximately)

Sift the flour into a large bowl and make a well in the center. Put the eggs, oil and salt into the well and mix with the fingers. Gradually work in the flour to form a crumbly dough. Knead to a firm but pliable dough, adding water as necessary.

Knead on a lightly floured board for 10 minutes or until smooth and elastic. Cover with a piece of oiled plastic wrap and let rest for 1 hour.

Roll out the dough on a lightly floured surface, rotating the dough a quarter turn after every roll until the dough is ⅛ inch thick. Shape and use as desired (opposite).

Green Pasta *(Pasta Verde)*
Follow the above recipe, adding ½ package (10-oz size) frozen chopped spinach (cooked and squeezed dry) with the eggs. This pasta is softer than plain pasta and frequent flouring of the work surface may be necessary.

Shaping Pasta

Stuffed Pasta: The dough should be used immediately, without drying.

Flat and Ribbon Pasta: Dust the dough lightly with flour and let dry for 15 to 20 minutes, but do not allow to become brittle. Cut flat pasta into shapes as pictured. Roll ribbon pasta into a loose jelly roll and cut across into strips as pictured.

Cooking Pasta

Homemade Pasta: Place the pasta in a large pot containing 3 to 4 quarts of boiling water and 1½ tablespoons salt. Stir well, and boil steadily, uncovered, for 3 to 5 minutes or until *al dente* – just tender but firm to the bite. Test frequently to avoid overcooking, as pasta continues to soften until you eat it. The moment it is done, thoroughly drain the pasta in a colander and serve immediately.

Dry Pasta: Follow the package directions. Cooking times are longer for dry pastas and vary considerably for different shapes and brands.

Never break up long pasta such as spaghetti; simply bend it into the pan as it softens.

Quantities

Allow 3 to 4 oz pasta per person for a main course, 2 oz for a first course.

Tagliolini con Tonno

1 can (7 oz) tuna
1 clove garlic,
 chopped
2 tablespoons
 chopped parsley
½ lb ripe tomatoes,
 peeled and
 chopped
⅔ cup chicken broth
Salt and pepper
¾ lb tagliolini

Drain the oil from the tuna into a small saucepan. Add the garlic and sauté for 2 minutes. Add the parsley and tomatoes and cook until the tomatoes begin to soften. Flake the tuna. Add it to the saucepan with the broth and salt and pepper to taste. Simmer while cooking the pasta.

Cook the pasta in boiling salted water until *al dente*; drain well. Toss with the sauce and serve immediately.

4 servings

Spaghetti alla Carbonara

¾ lb spaghetti
½ lb bacon, chopped
3 eggs
3 tablespoons heavy
 cream
½ cup grated
 Parmesan cheese
Salt and pepper
3 tablespoons butter

Cook the spaghetti in boiling salted water until *al dente*.

Meanwhile, cook the bacon until crisp. Drain well.

Beat the eggs with the cream, cheese, a little salt and plenty of pepper. Melt the butter in a large saucepan. Add the egg mixture and stir until just beginning to thicken. Add the drained spaghetti and bacon, mix well and serve immediately.

4 servings

Fettuccine al Gorgonzola

1 package (12 oz)
 fettuccine
2 tablespoons butter
5 tablespoons milk
¼ lb Gorgonzola
 cheese, diced
½ cup heavy cream
Salt and pepper
¼ cup grated
 Parmesan cheese
1 to 2 tablespoons
 chopped basil
 (optional)

Cook the pasta in boiling salted water until *al dente*.

Meanwhile, put the butter, milk and Gorgonzola into a large flameproof casserole. Place over moderate heat and mash the cheese to a creamy sauce. Add the cream and salt and pepper to taste and heat to the simmering point.

Stir in the drained pasta, Parmesan and basil. Toss just until the pasta is coated. Serve immediately with additional Parmesan.

4 servings

Lasagne al Forno

½ lb spinach
   lasagne
2 cups Rich Meat
   Sauce (page 14)
2½ cups Béchamel
   Sauce (page 16)
⅓ cup grated
   Parmesan cheese

Cook the lasagne in boiling salted water until *al dente*. Drain and rinse under cold water. Spread on clean dish towels and pat dry.

Butter a baking dish, at least 1½ inches deep. Spread a layer of meat sauce on the bottom, cover with a layer of lasagne, then meat sauce and finish with a thin layer of béchamel and a sprinkling of cheese. Repeat these layers twice, finishing with a final sprinkling of cheese.

Bake in a 400° oven 20 to 25 minutes, or until golden and bubbling.

4 servings

Tagliatelle alla Bolognese

¾ lb spinach
   tagliatelle
2 tablespoons butter
2 cups Rich Meat
   Sauce (page 14)
2 tablespoons grated
   Parmesan cheese

Cook the tagliatelle in boiling salted water until *al dente*. Drain thoroughly.

Melt the butter and pour into a deep serving dish. Add 4 tablespoons of the meat sauce, the pasta and Parmesan. Toss until the pasta is well coated. Spoon the remaining sauce over and pass more cheese separately to be sprinkled on top.

4 servings

Cannelloni

12 flat pieces
   homemade pasta,
   about 3 × 4 inches
   each
2 cups Béchamel
   Sauce (page 16)
Salt and pepper
1¼ cups Tomato
   Sauce (page 14)
3 tablespoons grated
   Parmesan cheese
2 tablespoons butter
FILLING:
2 tablespoons oil
1 onion, chopped
1 clove garlic,
   chopped
½ lb ground beef
1 package (10 oz)
   frozen chopped
   spinach
⅓ cup grated
   Parmesan cheese
1 egg yolk

Cook the pasta in boiling salted water until *al dente*, stirring occasionally. Drain, spread on a clean dish towel and pat dry.

To prepare the filling, heat the oil in a medium-size saucepan. Add the onion and garlic and sauté until softened. Add the meat and cook, stirring, until well browned. Squeeze the spinach dry and stir in with the remaining ingredients. Bind the mixture with 2 tablespoons of the béchamel and season well with salt and pepper.

Spread a heaped tablespoon of filling over each piece of pasta. Roll up loosely from the narrow side and place seam side down in a buttered baking dish.

Pour the tomato sauce over and cover with the béchamel. Sprinkle with the cheese; dot with the butter.

Bake in a 400° oven for 15 to 20 minutes, or until bubbling.

6 servings

Macaroni and Tomatoes
Macaroni con Pomodori

2 tablespoons oil
1 large onion, finely
  chopped
2 cloves garlic,
  chopped
1 small chili pepper,
  seeded and finely
  chopped
1 can (16 oz) crushed
  tomatoes
4 slices bacon,
  cooked and
  crumbled
1 teaspoon sugar
Salt
½ lb elbow macaroni
½ cup grated
  Provolone cheese

Heat the oil in a medium-size saucepan. Add the onion, garlic and chili pepper and cook until softened, stirring occasionally. Add the tomatoes, bacon, sugar and salt to taste. Bring to a boil, stirring; cover and simmer for 20 minutes.

Cook the macaroni in boiling salted water until *al dente*; drain thoroughly.

Arrange alternate layers of macaroni, sauce and cheese in a greased 2-quart baking dish, finishing with cheese.

Serve immediately, or cover and heat in a 275° oven for 20 to 30 minutes to allow the flavors to blend.

3 to 4 servings

Spinach-Stuffed Crepes
Crespelle Ripiene

CREPE BATTER:
1 cup all-purpose
    flour
¼ teaspoon salt
2 small eggs
1 tablespoon oil
¾ cup milk
6 to 8 tablespoons
    water
FILLING:
1 package (10 oz)
    frozen chopped
    spinach, cooked
1 cup ricotta cheese
1 egg, beaten
¼ cup grated
    Parmesan cheese
Grated nutmeg
Salt and pepper
TOPPING:
2 tablespoons butter
3 tablespoons grated
    Parmesan cheese
5 tablespoons
    chicken broth

To make the crepes, sift the flour and salt into a bowl. Make a well in the center and add the eggs, oil and milk. Beat until smooth. Stir in the water. Cover and chill for 1 to 2 hours.

Lightly oil a 7-inch crepe pan and place over moderate heat. When hot, pour in just enough batter to cover the bottom. When the crepe is set and the underside lightly browned, turn and lightly brown the other side. Repeat with the remaining batter, making eight crepes. (If not using the crepes immediately, stack with a piece of waxed paper between each crepe. Cover and refrigerate.)

Squeeze the spinach dry and combine with the filling ingredients, seasoning liberally with the nutmeg, salt and pepper. Divide among the crepes. Roll up loosely and arrange in a buttered baking dish. Dot with the butter, sprinkle with the Parmesan and pour in the broth.

Bake in a 400° oven for about 20 minutes or until the top is golden. Serve immediately.
4 servings

Home-Style Pizza
Pizza alla Casalinga

PIZZA DOUGH:
- 1 package active dry yeast
- 2 tablespoons warm water
- 2 cups all-purpose flour
- 1 teaspoon salt
- 2 tablespoons olive oil
- 6 tablespoons milk (approximately)

TOPPING:
- 3 tablespoons olive oil
- 1 can (16 oz) crushed tomatoes
- 1 teaspoon dried oregano or basil
- Salt and pepper
- ½ lb mozzarella cheese, sliced
- ¼ cup grated Parmesan cheese
- 6 to 8 ripe olives

Dissolve the yeast in the warm water. Sift the flour and salt into a bowl. Make a well in the center and pour in the yeast, oil and milk. Mix to a firm but pliable dough, adding a little more milk if necessary.

Place on a floured surface and knead vigorously for 5 minutes. Place in a greased bowl, cover and let rise in a warm place until doubled in bulk.

Knead the dough lightly. Cut in half. Roll each piece into an 8- to 9-inch round.

Place the rounds on oiled baking sheets and brush with some of the oil. Cover with the tomatoes and sprinkle with the herbs and salt and pepper. Add the mozzarella, then top with the Parmesan and olives.

Spoon the remaining oil over the pizza. Let rise in a warm place for 30 minutes.

Bake in a 425° oven for 25 to 30 minutes. Serve immediately.
4 servings

Individual Pizzas
Pizzette

1 recipe Pizza Dough
(opposite)
TOPPING:
3 tablespoons olive
oil
1 can (16 oz) crushed
tomatoes
Salt and pepper
1 cup sliced
mushrooms,
sautéed
2 to 3 cloves garlic,
finely chopped
2 to 3 tablespoons
grated Parmesan
cheese

Divide the risen dough into six portions. Shape into balls and roll into 4-inch rounds.

Place the rounds on oiled baking sheets and brush with half of the oil. Cover with the tomatoes and season well with salt and pepper.

Top with the mushrooms, garlic and cheese. Sprinkle with the remaining oil. Let rise in a warm place for about 15 minutes.

Bake in a 425° oven for about 15 minutes. Serve immediately.
6 servings

San Remo Pizza
Sardenara

1 recipe Pizza Dough
(opposite)
TOPPING:
7 tablespoons olive
oil
3 medium onions,
thinly sliced
1 to 2 cloves garlic,
minced
1 can (16 oz) crushed
tomatoes
1 teaspoon dried
oregano
Salt and pepper
1 can (2 oz) anchovy
fillets, cut into
strips
20 ripe olives

Prepare the dough as directed; set aside and let rise.

To make the topping, heat 4 tablespoons of the oil in a medium-size saucepan. Add the onions and cook until soft and golden. Add the garlic, tomatoes, oregano and a little salt and pepper. Simmer, uncovered, until reduced and thickened. Check the seasoning and let cool.

Place the risen dough on a floured surface and knead lightly. Cut in half. Shape each half into a ball and place the balls in well-oiled 8- or 9-inch foil pie pans. Press out the dough to cover the bottoms of the pans and to reach ½ inch up the sides. Brush with 1 tablespoon oil.

Spread the tomato mixture over the dough and arrange the anchovy strips and olives on top. Sprinkle the remaining oil over. Bake in a 425° oven for 25 to 30 minutes.
4 to 6 servings

MEAT

Steaks with Tomato Sauce
Bistecca alla Pizzaiola

4 individual sirloin
  steaks
Olive oil
Pepper
Fresh Tomato Sauce
  (page 15)
Salt

Brush the steaks with oil and season with pepper.

Lightly oil a large skillet and place over moderate heat. When hot, add the steaks and panfry quickly for 2 minutes on each side.

Spread the steaks with the sauce. Cover the skillet and cook over low heat for 5 to 10 minutes, or until the steaks are tender.

Transfer to a warmed serving platter, season with salt and garnish with herbs. Serve immediately.

4 servings

Florentine-Style Steak
Bistecca alla Fiorentina

1 T-bone or
   Porterhouse steak
   (1½ inches thick)
Salt and pepper
¼ cup olive oil
1 tablespoon lemon
   juice
1 tablespoon
   chopped parsley
1 clove garlic,
   chopped

Season the steak with salt and pepper. Place in a shallow baking dish and combine the remaining ingredients. Pour the marinade over the steak and refrigerate for 1 to 2 hours.

Drain the steak and place under a preheated broiler 3 inches from the heat. Broil 4 minutes on each side, or until the desired degree of doneness. Serve with lemon wedges.

4 servings

Roman-Style Beef Stew
Stufatino alla Romana

3 tablespoons butter
1 small onion, finely chopped
¼ cup finely chopped cooked ham
1 stalk celery, diced
1 clove garlic, sliced
1½ lb stewing beef, cut into cubes
¼ teaspoon dried marjoram
Salt and pepper
1 cup dry red wine
2 cups beef broth
1 tablespoon tomato paste
1 large bunch celery, cut into 2-inch lengths

Melt the butter in a large skillet. Add the onion and sauté until transparent. Add the ham, diced celery and garlic and cook for 1 minute. Add the beef, marjoram, salt and pepper; cook for 2 minutes.

Add the wine; boil until reduced by half. Add 1½ cups of the broth and the tomato paste. Cover and simmer for 3 to 4 hours, or until the meat is tender and the sauce is thick and rich. Stir occasionally. Add the remaining broth if the sauce reduces too quickly.

Meanwhile, cook the celery in boiling salted water for 5 to 10 minutes, or until tender. Drain and add to the stew just before serving, or serve separately.
4 servings

Beef Braised in Wine

Stracotto

1 tablespoon oil
2 tablespoons butter
1 small onion,
  chopped
1 small carrot,
  chopped
1 stalk celery,
  chopped
1 beef round roast
  (about 3 lb)
1 cup dry red wine
1 cup beef broth
1 tablespoon tomato
  paste
1 sprig thyme
1 bay leaf
Salt and pepper

Heat the oil and butter in a flameproof 3-quart casserole. Add the onion, carrot and celery and sauté for 5 minutes.

Add the meat and brown quickly. Add the wine; bring to a boil and simmer until well reduced.

Add the broth, tomato paste, herbs and salt and pepper to taste. Bring to a simmer. Cover and bake in a 300° oven for 3 hours, or until tender.

Cut the meat into thick slices and arrange on a warmed platter; keep hot.

Discard the herbs from the casserole. If necessary, reduce the sauce to about ½ cup by boiling uncovered, stirring frequently. Check the seasoning and spoon the sauce over the meat.
8 servings

Oxtail Stew
Coda alla Vaccinara

2 tablespoons olive
   oil
2 cloves garlic,
   chopped
1 onion, chopped
2 stalks celery,
   chopped
1 carrot, chopped
2 to 3 lb oxtail
2 cups dry white
   wine
1 can (16 oz) crushed
   tomatoes
Salt and pepper

In a 4-quart Dutch oven, combine the oil, garlic, onion, celery and carrot. Sauté for 3 minutes. Add the oxtail and brown for 10 to 15 minutes.

Add the wine and tomatoes and cook, covered, in a 350° oven for 3 to 4 hours, or until the meat is tender.

Remove the oxtail to a warmed platter. Skim the sauce of grease. Serve the oxtail with the sauce.

2 or 3 servings

Pot Roast with Anchovies

Stracotto alla Certosina

1 tablespoon olive
  oil
1 slice bacon,
  chopped
1 beef round roast
  (4 to 5 lb)
1 large onion,
  chopped
1 can (2 oz) anchovy
  fillets
1½ cups red wine
1½ cups beef broth
1 tablespoon capers
1 clove garlic,
  minced

In a 5-quart Dutch oven, heat the oil
and bacon. Add the roast and brown.
Add the onion and brown.

Mash the anchovies to a paste in
their own oil. Smear the paste over
the roast and then add the remaining
ingredients.

Cover and cook in a 325° oven for
about 2½ hours, or until the meat is
tender. Add more broth if necessary.

Remove the roast to a warmed platter. Skim the sauce of fat and serve
separately.

6 servings

Roast Lamb with Rosemary
Abbacchio al Forno

1 leg of lamb
  (about 6 lb)
4 to 6 cloves garlic,
  sliced
1 tablespoon dried
  rosemary
Salt and pepper
1 tablespoon oil
⅔ cup dry white
  wine or chicken
  broth

Make small slits in the lamb and insert a piece of garlic into each. Season with rosemary, salt and pepper. Place on a rack in a roasting pan. Rub with oil.

Bake in a 350° oven for 2 hours. Place on a platter and keep hot.

Skim the fat from the pan juices. Add the wine and bring to a boil, stirring, until thickened. Strain into a sauceboat and serve with the meat.

6 to 8 servings

NOTE: If fresh rosemary is available, tuck a small sprig into the slits along with the garlic.

Lamb in Lemon Sauce
Abbacchio Brodettato

2 tablespoons butter
½ cup chopped
  cooked ham
1½ lb stewing lamb,
  cut into chunks
1 onion, chopped
2 tablespoons flour
Salt and pepper
¼ cup dry white
  wine or vermouth
1½ cups chicken
  broth
2 egg yolks
½ teaspoon grated
  lemon rind
2 tablespoons lemon
  juice
1 tablespoon
  chopped parsley
¼ teaspoon dried
  marjoram

Melt the butter in a 10-inch skillet. Add the ham, lamb and onion and sauté for 10 minutes, stirring frequently. Sprinkle in the flour and season with salt and pepper. Cook, stirring, for 1 minute.

Add the wine. Bring to a boil and boil until reduced by half. Add the broth and bring back to a boil, stirring. Cover and simmer for 45 minutes, or until the lamb is tender. Skim off any surface fat.

Beat together the egg yolks, lemon rind and juice and the herbs. Add 3 tablespoons of the cooking liquid and blend well. Add to the skillet and stir just until the sauce thickens; do not boil. Check the seasoning. Serve with noodles or new potatoes.

4 servings

Piquant Lamb Chops
Agnello Piccante

8 lamb shoulder
  chops
¼ cup olive oil
2 cloves garlic,
  chopped
2 tablespoons
  chopped parsley
1½ tablespoons
  capers, chopped
¾ teaspoon dried
  marjoram
Salt and pepper
1 tablespoon lemon
  juice

Place the chops in one layer in a glass baking dish. Spoon the oil over them and sprinkle with the garlic. Cover and marinate for 2 hours; turn once.

Strain the marinade into a 12-inch skillet; add the parsley, capers and marjoram and heat gently. Add the chops and brown 5 minutes on each side. Season with salt and pepper and sprinkle with the lemon juice. Cover and cook over low heat for 5 minutes.

Arrange the chops on a warmed serving platter with the pan juices spooned over them. Garnish with lemon wedges.

4 servings

Sorrento-Style Pork
Fettine di Maiale alla Sorrentina

2 tablespoons oil
1 clove garlic, halved
4 pork loin chops
Pepper
1 large green pepper,
  seeded and thinly
  sliced
1 can (8 oz) tomatoes
½ lb mushrooms,
  thinly sliced
Salt and pepper

Heat the oil and garlic in a 10-inch skillet. When the garlic browns, discard it.

Add the chops to the skillet and brown lightly on each side. Season with pepper. Cover and simmer for 15 minutes. Remove the chops and keep hot.

Add the green pepper and tomatoes with their juice to the skillet, stirring to break up the tomatoes. Cover and simmer for 15 minutes.

Stir in the mushrooms. Cover and simmer for 5 minutes. Season to taste with salt and pepper.

Return the chops to the skillet. Baste with the sauce and simmer for 5 minutes. Serve with the sauce spooned over the chops.

4 servings

Herbed Pork
Maiale alla Veneziana

1 boned pork loin
  (3 lb)
1 clove garlic,
  chopped
¼ teaspoon each
  dried sage,
  rosemary and basil
Salt and pepper
2 tablespoons oil
2 cups chicken broth
2 teaspoons
  cornstarch,
  dissolved in
  1 tablespoon
  water

Untie the meat and lay flat. Combine the garlic, sage, rosemary and basil. Spread the mixture over the inside of the meat. Season well with salt and pepper. Reroll the roast tightly and secure with string. Rub with salt and pepper.

Heat the oil in a 4-quart Dutch oven. Add the meat and brown on all sides. Bring the broth to a boil and pour over the meat. Cover and simmer for 2 hours, or until the internal temperature of the pork is 170°.

Remove the pork to a warmed platter. Skim the excess fat from the cooking liquid. Stir in the cornstarch and cook over low heat, stirring, until slightly thickened. Carve the meat into thick slices and spoon the sauce over them.

4 servings

Stuffed Breast of Veal

Petto di Vitello Ripieno

2 tablespoons oil
1 onion, chopped
1 package (10 oz)
    frozen chopped
    spinach, cooked
    and squeezed dry
½ lb pork sausage
1 egg, beaten
3 tablespoons grated
    Parmesan cheese
Salt and pepper
1 boned breast of
    veal with pocket
    (about 2 lb)
2 tablespoons butter

To make the stuffing, heat the oil in a large saucepan. Add the onion and cook until soft. Stir in the spinach, sausage, egg, cheese, salt and pepper. Stuff the veal with the mixture and sew up or skewer the opening.

Place in a 3-quart casserole and dot with the butter. Cover and bake in a 325° oven for 2 hours, turning once.

Remove the thread or skewers and slice the veal. Serve hot, with the pan juices poured over, or cold.

6 servings

Veal Cutlets with Cheese
Scaloppine alla Parmigiana

4 veal cutlets
   (about 1 lb)
Flour for coating
Salt and pepper
1 tablespoon oil
3 tablespoons butter
1 cup chopped
   prosciutto or
   cooked ham
2 tablespoons
   chopped parsley
¼ cup grated
   Parmesan cheese
¼ cup chicken broth

Place each cutlet between two pieces of waxed paper and pound to flatten. Season the flour with salt and pepper and use to coat the veal.

Heat the oil and butter in a large skillet. Add the veal and sauté for about 3 minutes on each side.

Combine the ham and parsley and spread over the veal. Sprinkle with the cheese.

Stir the broth into the pan juices and spoon a little over each portion. Cover and simmer gently for 5 minutes, or until the veal is tender and the cheese melted.

Place on a warmed platter and keep hot. Bring the pan juices to a boil and cook briskly until reduced. Pour over the veal.

4 servings

51

Stuffed Veal Rolls

Involtini di Vitello alla Napolitana

8 thinly cut veal cutlets (about 1 lb)
8 thin slices prosciutto or cooked ham
½ cup soft bread crumbs, soaked in milk and squeezed dry
3 tablespoons golden raisins
¼ cup pignoli or coarsely chopped walnuts
¼ cup grated Parmesan cheese
2 tablespoons chopped parsley
Salt and pepper
1 tablespoon olive oil
2 tablespoons butter
¾ cup dry white wine

Place the cutlets between two pieces of waxed paper and pound to flatten. Cover each with a slice of ham.

Combine the bread crumbs, raisins, nuts, cheese and parsley and season with salt and pepper. Divide among the cutlets. Roll up and secure each one with a wooden-pick.

Heat the oil and butter in a 10-inch skillet. Add the veal rolls and sauté until lightly browned. Pour in the wine. Cover and simmer, turning once, for 20 to 25 minutes, or until tender.

Place the rolls on a warmed platter and keep hot; remove the picks. Bring the pan juices to a boil, stirring, and cook briskly until well reduced. Spoon over the meat and serve immediately.

4 servings

Veal in Tuna Mayonnaise

Vitello Tonnato

1 boneless veal
    shoulder roast
    (about 2 lb)
1 carrot, halved
1 onion, halved
1 stalk celery, sliced
1 bay leaf
4 peppercorns
Salt
1¼ cups Tuna
    Mayonnaise
    (page 17)
Anchovy fillets
Capers

Put the meat in a saucepan just large enough to hold it. Add the carrot, onion, celery, bay leaf, peppercorns and 1 teaspoon salt. Add just enough water to cover. Bring slowly to a boil. Skim the surface. Cover and simmer for 1½ to 2 hours, or until tender. Let cool in the stock.

Drain the meat and slice. Spread half the tuna mayonnaise on a serving platter and arrange the meat slices on top. Spread the remaining mayonnaise over the meat, covering it completely.

Cover the platter loosely with foil and chill several hours or overnight.

Serve, topped with anchovies and capers, as an antipasto or main course.

4 to 6 servings

53

Sautéed Kidneys
Rognoncini Trifolati

1¼ lb veal or lamb
  kidneys
2 tablespoons
  vinegar
2 tablespoons oil
2 tablespoons butter
2 cloves garlic, finely
  chopped
2 tablespoons
  chopped parsley
1 tablespoon lemon
  juice
Salt and pepper

Cover the kidneys with cold water and add the vinegar. Soak for at least 30 minutes. Cut out the core and thinly slice the kidneys.

Heat the oil and butter in a large skillet. Add the garlic and kidneys. Sauté, stirring constantly, for 2 minutes. Add the parsley, lemon juice, salt and pepper. Cook, stirring, for 1 to 2 minutes, or until the kidneys are tender but juicy. Serve immediately.

4 servings

Meatballs in Tomato Sauce
Polpette alla Siciliana

2 slices bread, crusts
  removed, soaked
  in milk and
  squeezed dry
1 lb lean ground beef
2 cloves garlic,
  minced
1 tablespoon
  chopped parsley
1 teaspoon grated
  lemon rind
¼ cup grated
  Parmesan cheese
Grated nutmeg
Salt and pepper
2 eggs, beaten
Flour for coating
Oil for frying
1¼ cups Tomato
  Sauce (page 14)

Place the bread, beef, garlic, parsley, lemon rind, cheese, nutmeg, salt and pepper in a large bowl. Add the eggs and mix lightly but thoroughly. Gently shape into 1½- to 2-inch balls. Roll the balls lightly in the flour. Chill until ready to cook.

Pour the oil into a 10-inch skillet to a depth of ¼ inch and place over moderate heat. When hot, add the meatballs, a few at a time, and sauté for 3 to 4 minutes, turning, until brown on all sides. Lift out and drain on paper towels. Pour off the fat, leaving any residue in the pan.

Add the tomato sauce to the skillet and thin to a pouring consistency with water if necessary. Return the meatballs to the skillet, stir gently and simmer for 15 to 20 minutes, or until cooked through.

4 servings

Venetian Liver and Onions

Fegato alla Veneziana

6 tablespoons butter
1 large onion, thinly
   sliced
Flour
Salt and pepper
2 lb calf's liver, cut
   into ½-inch slices
¼ cup wine vinegar

In a 10-inch skillet, melt 4 tablespoons of the butter. Add the onion and sauté until browned. Remove and set aside.

Season the flour with salt and pepper and lightly coat the liver. Melt the remaining butter in the skillet and quickly brown the liver on both sides. Return the onion to the pan and add the vinegar. Cook 2 minutes. The liver should still be pink in the center.

Serve on a warmed platter. Garnish with chopped parsley if desired.
4 to 6 servings

POULTRY

Chicken with Rosemary
Pollo con Rosmarino

1 chicken (2½ to
   3 lb), cut up
Salt and pepper
¼ cup oil
4 tablespoons butter
1 teaspoon dried
   rosemary
3 cloves garlic,
   crushed
½ cup dry white
   wine or chicken
   broth

Season the chicken with salt and pepper. Heat the oil, butter, rosemary and garlic in a large skillet. Add the chicken pieces and cook for 10 to 12 minutes, or until golden, turning once.

Add the wine. Bring to just below the boiling point. Simmer, uncovered, for 20 to 30 minutes, or until the chicken is tender. Place on a warmed platter and keep hot.

Remove the garlic and spoon the excess fat from the skillet. Add 2 to 4 tablespoons of water to the remaining pan juices. Bring to a boil, stirring well. Pour over the chicken.

4 servings

Chicken Breasts with Lemon

Petti di Pollo al Limone

2 whole chicken
  breasts, skinned
  and boned
Flour for coating
Salt and pepper
1 tablespoon oil
5 tablespoons butter
2 tablespoons lemon
  juice
3 tablespoons
  chicken broth
3 tablespoons
  chopped parsley

Halve the breasts and cut each horizontally into two slices. Season the flour with salt and pepper and use to coat the chicken slices.

Heat the oil and 3 tablespoons of the butter in a large skillet. Add the chicken and sauté for 5 to 6 minutes on each side, or until cooked through. Place on a warmed serving platter; keep hot.

Add the lemon juice and broth to the pan juices. Bring to a boil, stirring, and boil for 1 minute. Add the parsley and remaining butter and stir until blended. Pour the sauce over the chicken and serve immediately.

4 servings

Chicken with Peppers
Pollo con Peperoni

Flour for coating
Salt and pepper
1 chicken (2½ to
  3 lb), cut up
3 tablespoons oil
1 onion, thinly sliced
1 clove garlic,
  chopped
¼ cup dry vermouth
¼ teaspoon dried
  marjoram
1 can (8 oz) tomatoes
1 teaspoon sugar
1 green pepper,
  seeded and sliced

Season the flour with salt and pepper and use to coat the chicken. Heat the oil in a 12-inch skillet. Add the onion and chicken and sauté for 10 minutes, until golden. Pour off the oil.

Add the garlic, vermouth and marjoram to the skillet. Simmer until the wine has almost evaporated. Add the tomatoes with their juice, the sugar and green pepper. Cover and simmer for 30 minutes. Transfer the chicken to a warmed platter and keep hot.

Boil the sauce briskly, uncovered, until reduced and thickened. Check the seasoning and spoon over the chicken to serve.

4 servings

Chicken in Lemon Sauce
Pollo con Salsa d'Uovo

1 chicken (2½ to
  3 lb), cut up
Salt and pepper
2 tablespoons oil
2 tablespoons butter
¼ cup flour
1¼ cups chicken
  broth
1 bay leaf
Pinch of dried
  marjoram
2 egg yolks
1 tablespoon lemon
  juice

Season the chicken with salt and pepper. Heat the oil and butter in a 12-inch skillet. Add the chicken and sauté until golden. Remove and set aside. Pour off all but 2 tablespoons of the fat.

Add the flour to the skillet and cook, stirring, for 1 minute. Add the broth and bring to a boil, stirring. Return the chicken to the skillet and add the bay leaf and marjoram. Cover and simmer for 30 minutes.

Place the chicken on a warmed serving platter. Discard the bay leaf. Blend the egg yolks and lemon juice with 3 tablespoons of the sauce. Add to the skillet and heat gently, stirring, until thickened; do not boil. Pour the sauce over the chicken. Garnish with chopped parsley and lemon slices.

4 servings

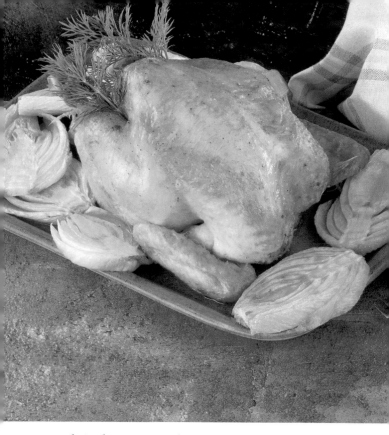

Chicken with Ham and Fennel
Pollo in Porchetta

1 chicken (3½ lb)
Salt and pepper
½ lb cooked ham,
  cut into thick
  strips
2 tablespoons
  chopped fennel
2 cloves garlic,
  crushed
3 tablespoons butter,
  softened
Lemon juice

Season the chicken inside and out with salt and pepper. Combine the ham, fennel and garlic. Stuff the chicken with the mixture. Rub the chicken all over with the butter and place in a small roasting pan.

Cover and bake in a 375° oven for 1 hour. Uncover and continue roasting, basting frequently, for 30 to 45 minutes, or until tender and golden brown. Place on a warmed platter and keep hot.

Season the juices with salt, pepper and lemon juice to taste and reheat. If desired, serve the chicken with Tuscan-Style Fennel (page 72). Pass the sauce separately.

4 servings

Tuscan Broiled Chicken

Pollo al Diavolo

1 chicken (2½ to
   3 lb), split
Salt and pepper
3 tablespoons olive
   oil
2 tablespoons lemon
   juice
2 cloves garlic,
   crushed
6 sage leaves,
   (optional)

Season the chicken liberally with salt and pepper.

Combine the remaining ingredients in a shallow glass dish. Add the chicken halves, turning to coat. Cover and marinate in the refrigerator for 4 hours, turning once.

Place the chicken skin-side down in a broiling pan. Broil 5 to 6 inches from the source of heat for 15 minutes. Turn and broil 15 minutes longer. Baste frequently with the marinade while broiling.

Place on a warmed platter and pour the pan juices over the chicken.

4 servings

Cornish Hens in Marsala
Gallina al Marsala

4 Cornish hens
   (about 1 lb each)
1/4 cup olive oil
2 tablespoons butter
1/2 teaspoon dried
   sage
Salt and pepper
1 1/4 cups Marsala
Juice of 1 small
   lemon
1/2 cup pitted green
   olives

Wash the hens under cold running water and pat dry with paper towels. Heat the oil and butter in a 5-quart Dutch oven. Add the hens and brown on all sides. Remove from the heat and add the sage, salt and pepper. Pour in the Marsala.

Cover and bake in a 350° oven for 50 minutes to 1 hour, basting several times with the pan juices and adding more Marsala if necessary. Remove the hens to a warmed serving platter.

Skim the excess fat from the cooking liquid. Place the Dutch oven over medium heat and stir in the lemon juice and olives. Warm just to heat through. Pour the sauce over the hens. Serve immediately. Garnish with sage leaves if desired.

6 servings

Chicken Cacciatora
Pollo alla Cacciatora

1 chicken (3 to
   3 1/2 lb), cut up
Salt and pepper
1/4 cup olive oil
1 onion, chopped
1/2 lb mushrooms,
   sliced
2 cloves garlic,
   chopped
1 teaspoon dried
   basil
1 can (16 oz) whole
   tomatoes,
   chopped
1/2 cup dry white
   wine
2 tablespoons
   chopped parsley

Season the chicken well with salt and pepper. Heat the oil in a 12-inch skillet. Add the chicken and brown well on all sides. Remove the chicken and set aside.

Add the onion, mushrooms and garlic to the skillet and cook until softened. Add the basil, tomatoes and wine and stir well. Bring to a boil. Lower the heat and add the chicken. Cover and cook for 25 minutes, or until the chicken is tender.

Remove the chicken to a warmed serving platter. Bring the sauce to a boil and boil vigorously until slightly reduced and thickened. Spoon the sauce over the chicken and garnish with the chopped parsley.

4 servings

Turkey Breast with Marsala

Filetti di Tacchino al Marsala

Flour for coating
Salt and pepper
1 turkey cutlet
　(about 1½ lb), cut
　into 4 slices
1 tablespoon oil
5 tablespoons butter
1 cup thinly sliced
　mushrooms
1 teaspoon lemon
　juice
2 tablespoons grated
　Parmesan cheese
6 tablespoons
　Marsala
2 tablespoons
　chicken broth

Season the flour with salt and pepper; coat the turkey with the mixture. Heat the oil and 3 tablespoons of the butter in a large skillet. Add the turkey and sauté for 4 to 5 minutes on each side. Place on a warmed serving platter and keep hot.

Melt the remaining butter in the skillet. Add the mushrooms and sauté for 3 minutes. Add the lemon juice and a little salt and spread over the turkey cutlets. Sprinkle with the Parmesan cheese.

Add the Marsala and broth to the skillet and boil rapidly, stirring, until reduced by half. Spoon over the turkey. Delicious accompanied with broccoli spears.

4 servings

NOTE: Chicken cutlets may be used instead of turkey.

Turkey with Ham and Cheese

Filetti di Tacchino alla Valdostana

Flour for coating
Salt and pepper
1 turkey cutlet
   (about 1½ lb), cut
   into 4 slices
1 egg, beaten
2 tablespoons oil
2 tablespoons butter
4 slices cooked ham
4 slices Bel Paese or
   mozzarella cheese

Season the flour with salt and pepper. Coat the turkey with the flour, then dip into the egg to coat. Heat the oil and butter in a large skillet. Add the turkey and sauté for about 4 minutes on each side. Drain and transfer to a broiler pan.

Cover each turkey slice with a slice of ham and then with cheese. Broil for 1 minute, or until the cheese is golden and bubbly. Serve immediately.

4 servings

NOTE: Chicken cutlets may be used instead of turkey.

FISH & SHELLFISH

Broiled Jumbo Shrimp
Spiedini di Scampi

1½ lb shrimp, peeled
and deveined
¼ cup olive oil
⅔ cup dry white
bread crumbs
2 cloves garlic,
crushed
1 tablespoon finely
chopped parsley
Salt and pepper
Lemon wedges

Put the shrimp in a bowl with the oil, bread crumbs, garlic, parsley and salt and pepper to taste. Stir to coat thoroughly. Cover and marinate for about 30 minutes.

Thread onto four skewers, pushing the shrimp to the center. Broil under a preheated broiler for 2 to 3 minutes on each side, depending on size, until the crumbs are crisp. Serve immediately, with lemon wedges.

4 servings

Shrimp with Garlic Butter
Scampi alla Griglia

2 lb jumbo shrimp
3 cloves garlic, minced
¾ cup olive oil (approximately)
1 tablespoon minced parsley
Juice of ½ lemon
Lemon wedges

Slit each shrimp down the back without removing the shell. Flatten and place cut side up in a shallow broiler pan. Sprinkle with the garlic and olive oil and put under a preheated broiler.

Broil 3 minutes, then turn the shrimp. Broil an additional 4 minutes, or until the flesh is opaque and the shrimp are cooked through.

Transfer to a warmed platter. Pour the cooking liquid over the shrimp and sprinkle with the parsley and lemon juice. Garnish with lemon wedges.

4 servings

Italian Fish Mayonnaise

Maionese di Pesce

1½ lb sole or other
   white fish fillets
1 lemon
3 to 4 tablespoons
   olive oil
Salt and pepper
1 package (10 oz)
   frozen mixed
   vegetables
1 package (5 oz)
   frozen cooked
   peeled baby
   shrimp, thawed
¾ cup Mayonnaise
   (page 16)

Put the fish in a large saucepan and cover with cold water. Add 2 lemon slices and poach for 5 minutes, or until cooked. Drain and chop the fish. While still hot, flavor to taste with oil, salt, pepper and lemon juice. Cover and let cool.

Cook the vegetables as directed on the package. Drain and cool. Place on a serving plate and top with the fish and half the shrimp. Pour the mayonnaise over, thinning with water if necessary. Sprinkle with the remaining shrimp. Decorate with hard-cooked eggs, stuffed olives and capers if desired.

4 servings

Golden Baked Fish
Pesce Gratinato al Forno

¼ cup olive oil
1 clove garlic, crushed
¼ teaspoon each dried mint and oregano
4 cod, hake or haddock steaks
Salt and pepper
⅔ cup dry bread crumbs
½ cup grated Parmesan cheese

Combine the oil, garlic, mint and oregano in a shallow glass dish. Season the fish lightly with salt and pepper and place in the marinade, turning to coat. Cover and marinate in the refrigerator for 3 to 4 hours, turning once. Drain, reserving the marinade.

Combine the bread crumbs and cheese and coat the fish, pressing on firmly.

Strain the marinade into a 10 × 6-inch baking dish and add the fish. Spoon enough marinade over to moisten the coating. Bake in a 375° oven for 20 to 25 minutes. Garnish with lemon wedges and herbs.

4 servings

69

Trout with Mushrooms

Trotelle alla Savoia

Flour for coating
Salt and pepper
4 lake trout, cleaned
2 tablespoons oil
5 tablespoons butter
3 green onions
  (green part only),
  chopped
¾ lb button
  mushrooms
1 tablespoon lemon
  juice
1 tablespoon
  chopped parsley
⅓ cup dry bread
  crumbs

Season the flour with salt and pepper and use to coat the trout.

Heat the oil and 2 tablespoons of the butter in a large skillet. Add the trout and sauté for 6 minutes on each side, or until cooked and golden.

Meanwhile, melt the remaining butter in a medium-size saucepan. Add the green onions and the mushrooms and sauté for 3 minutes, or until the mushrooms begin to soften. Stir in the lemon juice, parsley and a little salt.

Arrange the trout and mushroom mixture on a platter and keep hot.

Quickly sauté the bread crumbs in the butter remaining in the saucepan until crisp. Sprinkle over the fish.

4 servings

Sole with Zucchini

Sogliola all' Italiana

¼ cup oil
1 onion, finely chopped
½ lb tomatoes, peeled and chopped
1 teaspoon tomato paste
½ teaspoon dried basil
Salt and pepper
1 lb zucchini, thinly sliced
Flour for coating
4 sole fillets (about 1½ lb)
2 tablespoons butter
2 tablespoons grated Parmesan cheese

Heat half the oil in a 10-inch skillet. Add the onion and sauté until soft. Add the tomatoes, tomato paste, basil and a little salt and pepper. Simmer, covered, for 5 minutes. Add the zucchini and simmer for 8 minutes longer, or until just tender.

Season the flour with salt and pepper and use to coat the fish. Heat the remaining oil with the butter in a 12-inch skillet. Add the fish and sauté for 5 to 6 minutes on each side, or until cooked and golden.

Transfer to a shallow 11 × 7-inch baking dish and top with the vegetable mixture. Sprinkle with the cheese and broil until lightly browned.

4 servings

VEGETABLES & SALADS

Tuscan-Style Fennel
Finocchio alla Toscana

1¼ lb fennel bulbs
Salt
1 thick slice lemon
2 tablespoons oil
2 tablespoons butter, melted
Pepper
¼ cup grated Parmesan cheese

Trim the fennel bulbs and remove any discolored skin with a potato peeler. Cut vertically into ¾-inch-thick pieces. Place in a saucepan with a pinch of salt, the lemon and oil and enough boiling water to cover. Cook for 5 to 10 minutes, or until tender. Drain well.

Combine the butter and fennel in a shallow 1-quart baking dish; toss lightly to coat. Season to taste with pepper and sprinkle with the cheese.

Place under a preheated broiler and broil until lightly browned. Garnish with fennel leaves if desired.

4 servings

Peppers with Tomatoes

Peperonata

¼ cup oil
1 large onion,
    chopped
2 cloves garlic,
    chopped
2 bay leaves
6 large green
    peppers, halved
    and seeded
1 can (16 oz) crushed
    tomatoes
Salt and pepper

Heat the oil in a 10-inch skillet. Add the onion, garlic and bay leaves and sauté for 5 minutes, stirring occasionally, until softened.

Cut the peppers into ½-inch strips and add to the skillet; stir lightly. Cover and cook over low heat for 10 minutes.

Add the tomatoes and simmer uncovered, stirring frequently, until most of the liquid has evaporated and the mixture is fairly thick. Remove the bay leaves and season to taste with salt and pepper.

Serve hot with broiled chicken, chops or steaks, or cold as an antipasto.

4 servings

Spinach Mold
Sformata di spinaci

4 tablespoons butter
1 onion, grated
2 packages (10 oz each) frozen chopped spinach, thawed
¼ cup flour
1 cup milk
¼ cup grated Parmesan cheese
3 eggs, separated
Salt and pepper
Grated nutmeg
1¼ cups Tomato Sauce (page 14)

Melt half the butter in a 10-inch skillet. Add the onion and sauté for 5 minutes. Stir in the spinach, cover and cook for 5 minutes. Uncover and cook, stirring, just until all the moisture has evaporated.

Melt the remaining butter in a 2-quart saucepan. Add the flour and cook, stirring until browned. Add the milk and cook, stirring, for 2 minutes or until thick and smooth. Remove from the heat and beat in the cheese, egg yolks and spinach; add salt, pepper and nutmeg to taste.

Beat the egg whites until stiff and fold into the mixture. Spoon into a well-buttered 1½-quart ovenproof bowl or casserole and cover with buttered foil. Place in a roasting pan in about 1 inch boiling water. Bake in a 350° oven for about 1 hour or until firm in the center.

Let stand for 5 minutes, then invert onto a warmed platter. Serve with the sauce poured over the mold.
4 servings

White Beans with Tomatoes

Fagioli alla Toscana

2 cans (16 oz each) cannellini beans (see note)
3 tablespoons olive oil
2 cloves garlic, crushed
½ teaspoon dried sage
1 can (8 oz) whole tomatoes, drained and chopped
Salt and pepper

Rinse the beans with cold water and drain.

Heat the oil, garlic and sage slowly in a large saucepan for 1 to 2 minutes. Stir in the beans.

Add the tomatoes with salt and pepper to taste and stir gently. Cover and simmer for 10 minutes.

Serve hot as a vegetable, or cold topped with tuna as an antipasto.

4 servings

NOTE: If cannellini beans are unobtainable, cover 1 cup dried white beans with boiling water and soak overnight. Next day, simmer gently for 1½ to 2 hours, or until tender. Drain and use as directed above.

Cheese-Stuffed Zucchini

Zucchini Ripieni

3 zucchini (about 5 inches long)
2 slices white bread, crusts removed, soaked in 2 tablespoons milk
½ cup ricotta or cottage cheese
⅓ cup grated Parmesan cheese
1 clove garlic, minced
¼ teaspoon dried oregano
1 egg yolk
Salt and pepper

Parboil the zucchini in boiling salted water for 5 minutes; drain. Cut in half lengthwise and scoop out the centers; chop finely. Reserve the shells.

Squeeze the bread dry, reserving the liquid. Mix with the chopped zucchini, ricotta and Parmesan cheeses, garlic, oregano and egg yolk. Add a little milk if necessary to give a spreading consistency. Add salt and pepper to taste.

Fill the zucchini shells with the mixture and arrange in a well-oiled 10 × 6-inch baking dish.

Bake in a 375° oven for 35 to 40 minutes, or until tender and golden.

6 servings

Stuffed Mushrooms
Funghi Ripieni

12 large mushrooms
5 to 6 tablespoons
  olive oil
1 large onion,
  chopped
1 clove garlic,
  chopped
1 cup soft bread
  crumbs
½ cup diced cooked
  ham
2 tablespoons
  chopped parsley
2 tablespoons grated
  Parmesan cheese
Salt and pepper

Remove the stems from the mushrooms and chop finely. Heat 3 tablespoons of the oil in a small skillet. Add the onion, garlic and chopped mushroom stems and sauté gently for 5 minutes. Add the bread crumbs and cook until crisp. Stir in the ham, parsley, cheese and salt and pepper to taste.

Arrange the mushroom caps hollow-sides up in a greased shallow baking dish. Fill with the stuffing and sprinkle with a little oil.

Cover loosely with foil. Bake in a 375° oven for 25 minutes.

Serve hot, as an appetizer or as a side dish with chicken, meat or fish.

4 servings

Potato Dumplings
Potato Gnocchi

1½ cups all-purpose
  flour, sifted
1 egg, beaten
Salt and pepper
Grated nutmeg
1 lb potatoes, cooked
  and mashed
2 tablespoons butter
¼ cup grated
  Parmesan cheese
Chicken Liver Sauce
  or Meat Sauce
  (pages 12 and 13)

Combine the flour, egg and salt, pepper and nutmeg to taste with the potatoes. Mix well to form a firm dough. With floured hands, shape pieces of the dough into long rolls, about ½ inch thick. Cut into ¾-inch lengths; shape into curves around the little finger.

Cook in batches, by dropping into a large pot of boiling salted water and simmering for 3 to 5 minutes, or until they rise to the surface. Remove with a slotted spoon and drain. Place in a buttered shallow baking dish. Dot with the butter and sprinkle with the Parmesan. Bake in a 400° oven for 7 to 10 minutes.

Serve with the sauce poured over the dumplings.

6 servings

Eggplant Casserole
Melanzane alla Parmigiana

1 eggplant (about
   1½ lb)
Salt
Flour for coating
6 tablespoons olive
   oil
1¼ cups Tomato
   Sauce (page 14)
¼ lb mozzarella or
   Bel Paese cheese,
   thinly sliced
Pepper
3 tablespoons grated
   Parmesan cheese

Cut the eggplant lengthwise into ¼-inch slices. Sprinkle with salt and place in a colander. Let stand for 1 hour. Pat dry with paper towels. Coat lightly with flour.

Heat half the oil in a large skillet. Add half the eggplant slices and sauté until lightly browned on both sides. Remove with a slotted spoon and drain on paper towels. Repeat with the remaining oil and eggplant slices.

Arrange alternate layers of eggplant, tomato sauce and mozzarella in a greased 1½-quart casserole, sprinkling each layer with pepper and Parmesan and finishing with the Parmesan.

Bake in a 400° oven for 25 to 30 minutes, or until golden.

4 servings

Mixed Salad
Insalata Mista

Raw young spinach leaves are widely used for salads in Italy. When available, they make a nice change from lettuce. For a really crisp salad, after washing and thoroughly drying the lettuce or spinach, place in a plastic bag and chill in the refrigerator for a few hours.

1 head lettuce or
  ¼ lb young
  spinach leaves
½ green pepper,
  seeded and sliced
2 tomatoes, sliced
½ cucumber, sliced
6 radishes, sliced
DRESSING:
3 tablespoons olive
  oil
1 tablespoon lemon
  juice
1 clove garlic,
  minced
Salt and pepper

Tear the lettuce or spinach leaves into pieces. Place in a salad bowl and top with the remaining vegetables.

Combine the dressing ingredients in a screw-top jar, adding salt and pepper to taste, and shake well.

Just before serving, sprinkle the dressing over the salad and toss lightly.
4 servings

Fennel Salad
Insalata di Finocchio

1 large fennel bulb
½ cucumber, diced
4 radishes, sliced
2 oranges, divided
  into segments
DRESSING:
2 tablespoons olive
  oil
2 teaspoons lemon
  juice
1 clove garlic,
  minced
2 teaspoons chopped
  mint
Salt and pepper

Trim the stalks, base and coarse outer leaves from the fennel. Cut lengthwise into thin slices, then into strips. Place in a salad bowl with the cucumber, radishes and orange segments.

Combine the dressing ingredients in a screw-top jar and shake well. Sprinkle over the vegetables and toss lightly. Serve immediately.
4 servings

Cauliflower Salad
Insalata di Rinforza

---

1 cauliflower,
   broken into
   flowerets
5 tablespoons olive
   oil
1½ tablespoons
   wine vinegar
Salt and pepper
1 tablespoon capers
1 tablespoon
   chopped parsley
Few ripe olives
1 can (2 oz) anchovy
   fillets, drained and
   sliced

Cook the cauliflower in boiling salted
water for 5 to 6 minutes, or until
cooked but firm. Drain and rinse under
cold running water.

Mix the oil, vinegar and a little salt
and pepper in a salad bowl. Add the
cauliflower and toss gently. Sprinkle
with the capers, parsley and olives.
Arrange the anchovy fillets in a lattice
pattern on top. Serve immediately.
4 servings

Rice Salad
Insalata di Riso

Let this recipe be your inspiration for ways to turn leftover rice and vegetables into a delicious salad. Add pimientos for color or anchovies for zing. Be creative!

1 ⅓ cups water
½ teaspoon salt
1 ⅓ cups instant rice
¼ cup olive oil
1 tablespoon wine vinegar
2 green onions, finely chopped
1 small green pepper, thinly sliced
Salt and pepper
¼ cucumber, diced
2 tablespoons chopped parsley
Lettuce leaves

Bring the water and salt to a boil in a saucepan. Add the rice, stir well, cover and remove from the heat. Let stand for 10 minutes, or until the liquid is absorbed. Fluff the rice with a fork.

Combine the oil, vinegar, green onions, green pepper and salt and pepper to taste in a bowl. Add the hot rice and toss thoroughly. Cover and let stand until cool.

Just before serving, stir in the cucumber and parsley. Line a salad bowl with lettuce leaves and spoon in the rice salad.

4 to 6 servings

DESSERTS

Melon with Strawberries
Melone con Fragoline

1 melon
Superfine sugar
1 pint strawberries
2 tablespoons
   Cointreau or
   Grand Marnier
Juice of ½ lemon

Cut a "lid" off the top of the melon and reserve. Scoop out the fruit with a melon baller, discarding the seeds. Reserve the shell. Sprinkle the melon balls with a little sugar, cover and chill until serving time.

Sprinkle the strawberries with the liqueur, lemon juice and sugar to taste. Cover and chill until serving time.

When ready to serve, combine the melon and strawberries. Spoon them into the melon shell and partially cover with the "lid". Garnish with mint leaves if desired.

4 servings

Stuffed Peaches
Pesche alla Piemontese

4 large firm peaches,
　halved and pitted
¾ cup macaroon or
　amaretti cookie
　crumbs
¼ cup sugar
3 tablespoons butter,
　softened
1 egg yolk
½ teaspoon finely
　grated lemon rind
Slivered almonds
　(optional)

Scoop a little fruit from the center of each peach half and place in a bowl.

Add the crumbs, sugar, 2 tablespoons of the butter, the egg yolk and lemon rind and beat until smooth.

Divide among the peaches, shaping the stuffing into a mound. Sprinkle with slivered almonds and dot with the remaining butter. Arrange in a buttered baking dish – do not crowd.

Bake in a 350° oven for 20 to 35 minutes. Serve warm or cold with cream.

4 to 8 servings

Zabaglione

4 egg yolks
¼ cup sugar
½ cup Marsala

Put the egg yolks and sugar in the top of a double boiler over – but not touching – boiling water. Beat in the Marsala. Continue beating until the mixture begins to thicken and doubles in volume. Spoon into wine glasses to serve. Accompany with cookies if desired.

4 servings

Cassata alla Siciliana

3 eggs
½ cup sugar
½ teaspoon finely grated lemon rind
1 teaspoon vanilla
¾ cup all-purpose flour, sifted
FILLING AND FROSTING:
2 cups ricotta cheese
½ cup sugar
¼ cup Cointreau
2 oz semisweet chocolate, finely chopped
¼ cup diced mixed candied fruit
1 tablespoon chopped almonds or pistachio nuts

Beat the eggs, ½ cup sugar, the lemon rind and vanilla together until thick and fluffy. Fold in the flour.

Pour into a greased 8 × 4-inch loaf pan. Bake in a 375° oven for 25 minutes, or until a pick inserted in the center comes out clean. Invert onto a wire rack to cool.

Beat the cheese and ½ cup sugar until smooth. Add 2 tablespoons of the Cointreau. Divide the mixture in half. Place one portion in the refrigerator. Add the chocolate, candied fruit and nuts to the other portion for the filling.

Cut the cooled cake horizontally into three layers. Place the bottom layer on a serving platter and sprinkle with 1 tablespoon Cointreau. Spread with half the filling. Cover with another layer and sprinkle with the remaining Cointreau. Spread the remaining filling over and top with the last layer. Gently press the cake together; refrigerate.

One hour before serving, remove the cake and the frosting mixture from the refrigerator. Spread frosting over the cake. Decorate with candied cherries, candied orange and lemon slices and chocolate shavings.

6 to 8 servings

Sponge Cake
Pan di Spagna

3 eggs, separated
1 cup sugar
1 cup cake flour
1½ teaspoons
   baking powder
¼ teaspoon salt
¼ cup hot water
1 teaspoon vanilla
1 teaspoon grated
   lemon rind

Beat the yolks until frothy. Add the sugar slowly, beating until the mixture forms a ribbon when the beaters are lifted, about 3 to 4 minutes.

Sift the flour, baking powder and salt and fold into the batter. Add the hot water, vanilla and lemon rind. Beat the egg whites until stiff peaks form and fold in.

Pour the batter into a greased 8-inch square pan. Bake in a 350° oven for 25 to 30 minutes, or until the top springs back when touched lightly.

Cool the cake on a rack before removing it from the pan.

Italian Rum Cake
Zuppa Inglese

3 egg yolks
¼ cup sugar
¼ cup flour
2 cups milk
Grated rind of ½
   lemon
Sponge Cake
   (above), sliced into
   3 layers
½ cup dark rum
⅓ cup Amaretto
   liqueur
½ cup chopped
   toasted almonds

In the top of a double boiler, beat together the yolks and sugar over simmering water. Slowly add the flour. Mix in the milk and lemon rind. Cook, stirring, until the custard coats a spoon.

Place one layer of the cake in a shallow serving dish. Sprinkle with half of the rum and top with a third of the custard.

Add a second cake layer and soak with the liqueur. Top with half of the remaining custard.

Add the last cake layer and top with the remaining ¼ cup rum. Cover with the last of the custard and sprinkle with the almonds.

Refrigerate, covered, and serve well chilled. Garnish with whipped cream before serving.

Almond and Apricot Cookies
Pastini di Mandorle

½ cup butter,
   softened
1 cup sugar
1 egg, beaten
⅛ teaspoon almond
   extract
2 cups all-purpose
   flour
1 teaspoon baking
   powder
1 tablespoon milk
   (approximately)
½ cup finely
   chopped almonds
2 tablespoons
   apricot jam

Cream the butter and sugar until light and fluffy. Beat in the egg and almond extract. Sift the flour and baking powder together and stir into the mixture with enough milk to make a smooth paste.

Roll teaspoonfuls of the mixture into balls. Roll in chopped almonds and place well apart on a greased baking sheet. Make a deep dent in the center of each and fill with jam. Bake in a 400° oven for 12 to 15 minutes, or until golden. Let stand for 5 minutes. Remove to a wire rack and cool. Store in an airtight container.
Makes about 3 dozen

Hazelnut Ice Cream
Gelato alla Nocciola

1 cup hazelnuts
1¼ cups milk
4 egg yolks
½ cup sugar
⅛ teaspoon vanilla
¾ cup heavy cream,
   whipped

Spread the nuts on a baking sheet and toast under a preheated broiler, shaking frequently until the skins split. Place the nuts in a towel and rub off the loose skins. Grind the nuts.

Place the milk in a small saucepan and bring almost to a boil. Cream the egg yolks, sugar and vanilla in a bowl until pale. Gradually stir in the milk. Stir in the ground nuts.

Pour into a clean saucepan. Heat gently, stirring, until the mixture is thick enough to coat the back of the spoon; do not allow to boil. Cover and let stand, stirring occasionally, until cold.

Fold in the whipped cream. Spoon into a freezer container; cover and freeze until firm.

Twenty minutes before serving, place in the refrigerator to soften.
4 or 5 servings

Strawberry Ice Cream
Gelato di Fragole

1 pint strawberries
Juice of ½ orange
2 teaspoons lemon
   juice
¾ cup powdered
   sugar
1 cup heavy cream
Halved strawberries,
   to decorate

Puree the strawberries in a blender, then strain. Stir in the orange and lemon juices and sweeten to taste with powdered sugar. Whip the cream until thick but not stiff. Gently fold in the strawberry mixture. Spoon into a freezer container; cover and freeze until firm.

Twenty minutes before serving, place in the refrigerator to soften. Spoon into individual dishes and decorate with strawberries.

4 servings

Orange Ice
Granita di Arancia

1 cup sugar
2½ cups water
1¼ cups orange juice
2 tablespoons lemon
    juice
1 teaspoon finely
    grated orange rind

Place the sugar and water in a small saucepan over moderate heat and stir until dissolved. Bring to a boil and boil for 5 minutes. Cool to room temperature. Stir in the fruit juices and orange rind.

Pour into an ice cube tray. Freeze until mushy, stirring every 30 minutes. Serve with a straw or spoon.
4 servings

NOTE: If the ice freezes solid, remove to the refrigerator to soften until it can be mashed with a fork.

Lemon Ice *(Granita di Limone)*
Substitute 1¼ cups fresh lemon juice for the orange and lemon juice and orange rind.

Amaretti Ice Cream Bombe

Gelato agli Amaretti

1 cup amaretti
   cookie crumbs
3 tablespoons
   Marsala or dry
   sherry
   (approximately)
1 pint vanilla ice
   cream

Mix the cookie crumbs with the Marsala to form a soft paste.

Soften the ice cream slightly. Spread two-thirds of the ice cream over the bottom and up the side of a 3-cup bowl. Spread the amaretti mixture in the center and cover with the remaining ice cream, smoothing the top. Cover with foil and freeze until firm.

Thirty minutes before serving, invert the bombe onto a serving plate and place in the refrigerator to soften. Decorate with whipped cream and amaretti cookies if desired.

4 servings

Siena-Style Nut Bread
Panforte di Siena

This flat "cake" with a nougatlike texture, rich with candied fruit, toasted nuts and spices, is a particular specialty of the town of Siena. Although it can be served as a dessert to complete a light meal, Italians would be more likely to serve it with coffee in the morning or mid afternoon.

¾ cup hazelnuts
¾ cup chopped almonds
1 cup chopped mixed candied fruit
¼ cup unsweetened cocoa
½ cup all-purpose flour, sifted
½ teaspoon ground cinnamon
¼ teaspoon apple pie spice
½ cup granulated sugar
⅓ cup honey
2 tablespoons powdered sugar
1 teaspoon ground cinnamon

Spread the hazelnuts on a baking sheet and toast under a preheated broiler, shaking frequently until the skins split. Place in a towel and rub off the skins. Coarsely grind the hazelnuts.

Combine the hazelnuts, almonds, candied fruit, cocoa, flour, ½ teaspoon cinnamon and the pie spice in a mixing bowl; stir well.

Combine the granulated sugar and honey in a large saucepan and heat gently until the sugar has dissolved. Boil until the mixture reaches a temperature of 240° on a candy thermometer, or forms a soft ball when a bit is dropped into a cup of cold water. Remove from the heat and stir in the dry ingredients.

Line an 8-inch springform pan with wax paper; butter the paper. Press the dough into the pan so that the mixture is no more than ¼ inch thick. Bake in a 300° oven for 30 to 35 minutes.

Remove from the pan and allow to cool. Peel off the lining paper and place the cake on a serving platter. Mix the powdered sugar with 1 teaspoon cinnamon and sift over the cake. Cut into wedges to serve.

8 to 10 servings

INDEX

Almond and apricot cookies, 88
Amaretti ice cream bombe, 91
Antipasto, 22, 23
Artichoke hearts, marinated, 24

Beans, white, with tomatoes, 75
Béchamel sauce, 16
Beef
    braised in wine, 43
    Florentine-style steak, 41
    meatballs in tomato sauce, 54
    pot roast with anchovies, 45
    oxtail stew, 44
    steaks with tomato sauce, 40
    stew, Roman-style, 42

Cakes
    cassata alla Siciliana, 84
    Italian rum, 86
    sponge, 86
Cannelloni, 35
Caponata, 24
Cassata alla Siciliana, 84
Cauliflower salad, 80
Cheese noodles in broth, 20
Chicken
    breasts with lemon, 57
    broth, 19
    cacciatora, 62
    in lemon sauce, 58
    Tuscan broiled, 61
    with ham and fennel, 60
    with peppers, 58
    with rosemary, 56
Chicken liver sauce, 12
Cookies, almond and apricot, 88
Cornish hens in Marsala, 62
Crepes, spinach-stuffed, 37

Desserts, 82-93

Egg soup, Roman, 18
Eggplant
    appetizer, 24
    casserole, 77
Eggs with tuna mayonnaise, 27

Fennel
    salad, 78
    Tuscan-style, 72
Fettuccine al Gorgonzola, 32
Fish, 66-71
    golden baked, 69
    mayonnaise, Italian, 68

Gnocchi, 76
Green sauce, piquant, 17

Hazelnut ice cream, 88

Ices, 90
Ice cream
    bombe, Amaretti, 91
    hazelnut, 88
    strawberry, 89

Kidneys, sautéed, 54

Lamb
    chops, piquant, 47
    in lemon sauce, 47
    roast, with rosemary, 46
Lasagne al forno, 34
Lemon ice, 90
Liver and onions, Venetian, 55

Macaroni and tomatoes, 36
Mayonnaise, 16
    Italian fish, 68
    tuna, 17
Meat sauce, 13, 14
Meatballs in tomato sauce, 54
Melon with strawberries, 82
Minestrone, 22
Mushroom and shrimp salad, 26
Mushrooms, stuffed, 76